animal coloring book for children

ages 4-8

Designed in 2020

a cow

bear

Cats

Dinosaur

Elephant

frog

giraffe

horse

rooster

Hen

chick

Duck

Parrot

monkey

squirrel

urchin

Tortoise

Sheep

loin

dog

Tiger

triceratops

Fish

starfish

crab

animal coloring book for children
ages 4-8

DESIGNED IN 2020